Letters To a
Mixed Race Son

5/22/13

By Frank E. Robinson, Jr.

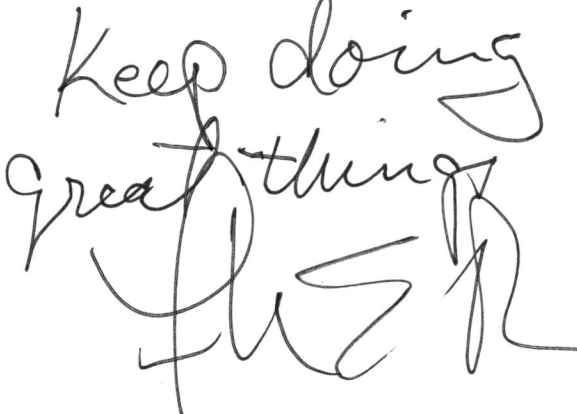

Keep doing great things

Frank E. Robinson, Jr.

Copyright © 2011 by Frank E. Robinson, Jr.
All Rights Reserved

To my son, Frank Gershom Robinson.
You are an arrow I took to my bow,
pointed to the target and let fly.

ACKNOWLEDGEMENTS

A note of special thanks to Mrs. Jerice Kenebrew, who urged me to publish these letters, then painstakingly typed from my handwritten pages. Sincere thanks also to all those who nurtured, encouraged, kindly scolded, provoked, nudged forward and supported this work. You are too many to name. To each of you I am deeply grateful.

FOREWORD

I have known Frank Robinson for decades. He is a thoughtful writer, an excellent artist, a devoted husband and father. He is a fine minister, with a sincere love for the Lord and for all people.

Frank crossed the tracks at an early age and did not look back or apologize. He married an African American woman in the Deep South, at a time when interracial marriages were not welcome, not approved and dangerous to the parties involved. He brings awareness, insight and sensitivity to the table.

During significant years in the life of West Angeles, Frank assisted me. Among other duties, he developed our Diversity Ministry, which was a tool to welcome, include and communicate our love to those who had crossed racial and cultural barriers to be with us.

Frank was at his desk in 1992 as the Rodney King beating verdicts were read, and Los Angeles erupted in flames and violence. In 1994 he was present for what became known as the "Miracle in Memphis." The Lord's hand is on this man.

The words in the book you hold in your hand are not

the words of a dilettante. It cost Frank something to be who he is. He is dyed-in-the-wool legit.

<u>Letters to a Mixed Race Son</u> allows us to look over the shoulder of a loving father, who clearly, deliberately and insightfully speaks life into the life of his son. We are so privileged.

Get this book. Give this book. Read these <u>Letters to a Mixed Race Son</u> for yourself. They are rich and beautiful, powerful and spiritual, ministry laden, profound and transcendent. Let the words of a loving father find a receptive heart. I am certain this book will bless and inspire you.

Bishop Charles E. Blake
Senior Pastor, West Angeles Church
Presiding Bishop, Churches of God in Christ

PREFACE

This book began as an investment I made in the life of my son. I thought it may have value to others.

When I was a young Christian, I had my life threatened and I confronted many dangerous situations recklessly. My thinking was simple, for if I die tonight, I will be with the Lord. This was extremely liberating to me and it freed me to do some exciting things.

But when I became a husband and father, I had to think differently. If someone succeeded in killing me, my wife would be a widow, and my children would be without a father. With a deepened awareness of my own mortality, I began to calculate my risks more carefully.

Not long after I left the South, I began to write letters to my son. I wanted to communicate my love to him and to say important things a father should say, even if we were separated by my death.

A father is powerful. There is such a narrow window of time, and, for better or worse, a father's presence or absence, his words and his silence, his actions and non-actions, all have profound effect on individuals, the family, community, nation and world, even across generations.

At this writing, my son is a young father. He is a military officer, preparing to go overseas to war in a few days. After about twenty five years of writing letters, I closed the book and recently put the hand written original in the hands of my son.

<u>Letters to a Mixed Race Son</u> is intended also for every father and mother, every son and daughter, every sister, brother, neighbor and friend. May this book inspire you to see the world differently, and maybe to be a better you.

Please take this book home and let it find that better you. Then, please, share the good you received with a world that needs to see dissimilar people love and respect each other. I think a generation and another generation may rise up and call you blessed.

Frank Robinson

November 5, 1986

Dear Son,
I have looked forward to begin a series of writings especially for you. As I write this, I can hear you turning in your baby bed. It's getting close to 2 AM. Hopefully, this will be a rewarding experiment. Maybe one day you will understand how much I love you.

I was there when you arrived, when you drew your first breath of air. Your first cries I heard, and even now your cry is similar to what I heard that day.

The God of heaven has brought us through many things and He has done great things for us. We have been quite poor, yet made quite rich. He has enriched us also by giving you to us, and we are thankful.

It is very late now, Son. I love you and I'm praying for you.

~Dad

November 5, 1986
(near midnight)

Dear Son,
I want to avoid the syrupy kind of renderings I have seen. We affectionately call you by your middle name, Gershom. Later in your life you may prefer to be called by your first name, Frank. The name Gershom is found in Exodus 2:22. Moses had fled for his life from Egypt to Midian, and married there. A son was born, and Moses named him Gershom, "... for he said, I have been a stranger in a strange land."

As you know, I am a Gospel minister. I desire to honor the God of my salvation in every aspect of my life. In 1984, I travelled from California to Alabama and ministered at the Prayer House Church in Brewton. It was January, and we had a glorious time.

The pastor of that church said he would like me to work with him. I said I'd pray about it, returned to California and spent days on my face, fasting and praying. There was a clear "Go to Alabama" in my heart. I tied up loose ends, paid my bills, put my books and clothes into my car, said goodbye to my family and friends -not knowing if I would ever see them again- and left for Alabama.

At that time, it was very unusual for churches to be racially integrated, especially in the South. Somehow, it seems, they have maintained the hypocrisy and sickness of their fathers. From the start, I was a controversial presence in Brewton.

I met your mother there. She was a faithful young saint, very dedicated, meek and prayerful. One day, the Lord spoke to my heart, that she was my wife. As a minister, with much to be considered, I prayed and sought God concerning this. There were common, recent reports that in one of the places where we had an outreach, a man had been decapitated and mutilated. He had been involved in an interracial relationship. There were other atrocities merely in the reputation of the South.

Then also, as a minister, I didn't want to make a wrong move…too much was at stake. I didn't want to damage my ministry, or get a reputation as a womanizer, so I prayed, prayed and prayed. But God had led us. I never had to ask her to marry me, and we were soon married.

I do not know if I can fully explain what a scandal it was, or what a notorious figure I had become. Strangely, I felt loved and even admired by some. But I also got a taste of being despised and rejected.

Your mother worked at the local medical center. When it became known that we were getting married, they changed toward her and treated her differently. When she was carrying you, I made a decision. A certain doctor in town had a bad and dangerous reputation. I was told that one baby died and another was disfigured by this man's hands. He sounded incompetent. Given that, along with the climate of public opinion, I decided that you would be born across the state line. I didn't want some doctor, trying to do society a favor, to kill you.

Gershom, a sojourner, an alien, here. Your father was a stranger in a strange land. This is true for you, also. This world is not your home. We are pilgrims, merely strangers passing through. Jesus has prepared a place for us in His Father's house. I want to meet you there.

Much love,
Dad

November 14, 1986
(Again, near midnight)

Dear Son,
Tonight you greeted me in your affectionate way. When you made your musical expression by patting your own legs, it again witnessed to a fact I already know. You love music and are developing some level of skill in that area. Also tonight, for the first time I can remember, you said "Jesus," plainly. I am so delighted with you.

I want to talk with you about identity.

People often go to great lengths becoming, or trying to be, something God never intended them to be. You may struggle with this also. Remember, no one else is you. As with others, God knows the number of hairs on your head, and he gives you choices daily.

One can go through life as an actor. You can live and die playing a part not intended for you. Granted, pressure may be upon you from here or there, but the choice, how you choose to be you, is a privilege God gives.

What kind of man will you be? Will you be foolish or wise? Weak, or strong? Shallow, or profound?

God had a purpose for you before He made the world. Seek the Lord early, and watch God work His plan. To others this may seem dull and stifling. But I promise you unsurpassed thrill and satisfaction if you give yourself fully to God.

You may choose an alternate route, and never taste the sweetness of these things. But those other ways are not for you, and if you linger, they will make a prisoner of you.

I invite you to follow me as I follow Jesus. Find your identity in Him. When He comes for us, you won't be ashamed.

Love always,
Dad

PS Because of the fact that your mother is black and I am white, a tremendous pressure may be put upon you. In terms of racial and social identity, be yourself, both your father's son and your mother's son. Let that person you are be hid in Christ. If you are loved, let them see Jesus, and if not, let them see Jesus. You will be a light in darkness.

Many days may bring occasion for you to rise up, and every fiber of your being may long to avenge an insult, an injury, an injustice. In that day, remember whose son you are. God is faithful. Never will He let you be tempted beyond your capacity, and He will always, always, always provide a way for you to escape. Be wise, my son, and my heart shall rejoice, even mine.

Dec. 6, 1986
12:16 AM

Dear Son,
The proverb says, "Hope deferred maketh the heart sick; but when the desire cometh, it is a tree of life." Proverbs 13:12

Disappointment has visited many. One day, and perhaps many days, you will taste disappointment. Maybe a dearly held dream is dashed to pieces before your eyes and you are helpless to repair it, or live that dream, ever. There are so many possibilities for disappointment ... but that is not what I want to dwell on here.

There are so many promises the God of Heaven has for you. They are for you, rightfully yours. As a wise man, set your affections on things above. Delight thyself also in the Lord; and he shall give thee the desires of thine heart.

Many times we must wait, and in our lives God's wisdom can be on display to the universe. During the waiting, your heart may cry out in agony and frustration, "Doesn't God see? Doesn't He hear? Doesn't He know?"

Be patient, my son. Surely He sees. Surely He hears. Surely He knows. He cares for you.

For a moment, the wrong way may seem right. Please remember that there is a way that seems right to a man, and the way of a fool is right in his own eyes. Ask for God's way, and walk in it. You may have to suffer, you may have to wait. But if you hold on to Christ, He will anchor your soul.

Delayed hope makes the heart ache. But, when God turns things around for you, it will be worth every price you paid, every moment and every heart beat you waited.

I love you so much,
Dad

Jan. 15, 1987
12:05 AM

Dear Son,
As you sleep, and as I prepare to do the same, I enjoy so much thinking of you. You are advancing so quickly, learning so much now. Honestly, I wish that our present financial situation was better, but this won't last forever.

I would like to give you so much more in several categories, even frustratingly simple things like pajamas and shoes that are more to your correct size. Here is another time we are close to the edge.

But, the Lord is faithful. When you or I have needed shoes, God provided them. When we needed food, He sent it. None of our basic needs are lacking. God is good. He never, ever abandoned us. Look around! Can you see His goodness, His kindness?

Son, what would you call success? How would you define it? What does it look like?

The Bible tells us of Enoch, who had family and responsibility, yet he walked with God in a sinful world. Enoch pleased God. This is the very essence of true and eternal success. Jesus prayed, "I finished the work You gave Me to do." Mission accomplished. I did what You said. I completed the task.

I want to please the Lord. I want to fulfill my God given purpose for being. If, at the end of your sojourn on this planet it can truthfully be said of you, "He pleased God," then Son, you will have been a great and a successful man, and I will be a grateful man.

Love,
Dad

Feb 9, 1987

Dear Gershom,
One of the most difficult things for some people to deal with successfully is criticism. A man's self esteem can be so delicate, so fragile, that he shrinks and withdraws from exposure to criticism.

Perhaps to a greater or lesser degree, we all encounter the penetrating arrows of the critic. But to some, criticism threatens, terrorizes and paralyzes them. Criticism tends to intimidate, hold them hostage, or in a state of retreat and surrender. What another man thinks or says can be a dark shadow that hides the sun of your day.

As I was growing up, I very much enjoyed drawing and art in general. It's a gift I worked hard to develop. The quality of my work was better than most of my peers and would often get noticed and complimented.

My father was not quite the painter I am, but he was one of the most creative people I ever met. My dad would see some of my work and point out areas that were weak or wrong, or in need of improvement, possibly a place where I had obscured a flaw.

Often, he was correct, and I used those observations constructively to become a better artist.

At art shows, I heard many comments on my work. Some were praising, others were utterly scathing. When you are out there, there is nowhere to hide. Listening to everything can be discouraging and confusing. So I divided my critics into two groups, those who know what they are talking about and those who do not. If the observations are valid and informed, they are beneficial and I can use them constructively. They will make me better. If the criticism is unfounded, what of it? How am I injured?

"Let the righteous smite me; it shall be a kindness: and let him reprove me; it shall be an excellent oil, which shall not break my head…" Psalm 141:5

Take advantage of informed and honest criticism. It can be of vast benefit to you, a means of improvement and growth. Yes, the words can hurt. They can sting like arrows. But there is no need to fear the truth.

With great love,
Dad

April 13, 1987
4:05 AM

Dear Son,
You are so rapidly growing and showing such advancement in your abilities and level of understanding. Have you noticed that I have written to you as a man, and as of this date, you are not yet two years old? I think my words will be more precious to you the older you become. I want to share some thoughts with you.

If you look around, you will see many people who have suffered many things, possibly through no fault of their own, and their present is greatly affected. Some are haunted, swallowed up by their own experiences. For many, the past drains life, meaning and joy out of their present. It robs and sabotages their future.

Most of us, or all of us, could look back and say that much of our present condition can be explained by our past. A man can say, "I wouldn't be like this if my parents had been different." Another can say, "If my home wasn't broken, if my father was not an alcoholic, I could have done better, I could have succeeded in life."

The helpless victim of circumstance says, "If only these things had not happened, I would not be this way."

I sympathize with the victim and I want to be a part of healing the bruised and broken hearted, to help unlock their chains.

But in my thinking, a man should reach a place where he does not point his finger at others, not his parents, his environment, or his past, saying "It is their fault I am what I am." A man cannot undo his past, but he can take responsibility for what he does with the present.

I can look at my parents, and then beyond to their parents, and beyond that, and see how our circumstances could be so different today, if only this and if only that were changed. I could avoid personal accountability and say that their failures contributed to and even caused my own failures.

But NO! I am a man and I make the choices of a man. How then can I honestly point at another and say, "His fault," or, "Her fault," when I make decisions, when I make choices in life? Surely, as a man, I cannot.

Frank E. Robinson, Jr.

You will have choices in life. Use them well. I'm praying for you. Make good decisions. Be a man among men.

Love,
Dad

Jan. 12, 1988

Dear Son,
At this date, you are about 2½ years of age.

A few days ago, I suffered a great financial loss. This may affect our family for years to come, but we will look up and keep on going. The Lord is our helper, and He will help us.

Also, a few days ago, an incident happened that I wish to share with you. While I was resting, you persisted in making noise, thus disturbing me. When finally things got to a point that I got up to correct you, my words were sharp and I began to speak with anger.

Then you did something I didn't expect. You came up to me, I may have been still talking, you put your arms around my neck and said, "Forgive me, Daddy!" Son, you surprised me. You disarmed me. You got to my heart again.

You are greatly loved,
Dad

April 17, 1988

Dear Frank Gershom,
My son, how I love you. The days run by so quickly. Now, as I write you, your brother and mother are asleep. In spite of all surrounding circumstances of poverty and doing without, the family provides a sweetness to my life.

I want to be transparent before you in these words, and your perception of me may be affected. But one day you may stand in my shoes.

Tonight I feel crushed, bruised and heartbroken. I have done good, told the truth, did not cheat, and yet now I endure grief and we suffer. It is unfair. It is unjust. It is prolonged.

At the word "crushed" I thought of a glass of wine or grape juice. Imagine with me, and hold the glass up to the light. As you turn the glass in your hand, you don't see the bruising or crushing of the grapes. Observe the sparkle, the color, the fragrance.

Now, consider again the grape. It was for this cup the cluster was cut off from the dew of morning and the full day of sun. For this cup the tender grapes were crushed. You are important and God has a purpose for you in His universe.

July 14, 1988

Dear Son,

As I write, the voice of your mother's praying is in my ears. You are now just past another birthday and I thank God for you.

Concerning the issue I spoke of earlier, I have found liberty in my spirit and freedom in my heart. I am willing, if it be the will of God, to suffer myself to be defrauded, to take wrong. I trust that God will cause me to triumph and that He will cause all things to work together for good. So, I rest in Him.

A man I met recently, who had suffered an injustice, had lost a home and vehicles. His heart was filled with such venom and thirst for revenge, that, while it destroys him, he may ultimately destroy others. He may end up a murderer.

I spoke with this man, but could not get far. Our lives are going in two different ways. He would not listen.

Son, remember the wisdom of the man who built on a rock. When the raging waters pass, that house will remain.

It is good to be free.

Love,
Dad

August 1, 1988

Dear Son,
When you read this, it may be that both of us have forgotten a thousand of the common, yet beautiful events of today. Your lovely mother shared with me something you did a few days ago and I want to share it with you.

At three years old, you sat on our couch with a toy phone. You were overheard as you pretended to talk to Jesus on your phone. The conversation went something like this, "I love you, and I just want to be with you, but I don't like this yellow stuff that keeps coming out of my eye." Again, the other day, you told me that you wanted to go to church, "To worship the Lord."

Son, if I fail you, please forgive me. I desire so much to give to you the foundation that I didn't have. I pray for wisdom and sensitivity and I observe that you are a sensitive and kind person. Be real.

Love,
Dad

August 25, 1988

Dear Son,

This morning my grandfather died. He was 94 years old. He lived in the house in front of the apartment we live in. My mother had been taking care of him for years. I was called this morning because he had stopped breathing. When I got there, it was evident that Grandpa had been dead for a while. His flesh was cold and his body had stiffened.

I tried to be of comfort to my mother, my niece and others, but I have so many thoughts and feelings to deal with as well. I outwardly display cool composure, yet inwardly, I wrestle.

Last night, as your great-grandfather was at the threshold of eternity, your cousin Jolie and I tossed and bounced a ball to him as he sat in his wheelchair. He bounced the ball back to us. For a moment, a measure of some past dexterity returned to him. The moment is gone forever.

In the morning, a shell, a house that we recognized remained. A person who preceded us was not there. Was the man saved? Only God is the judge. I came upon him once, as he was in bed, with his hands clasped, as in prayer.

The psalmist said, "We spend our years as a tale that is told…So teach us to number our days, that we may apply our hearts unto wisdom."

Perhaps one day, my grandson or your grandson will find comfort when we depart from this world, knowing in his heart that we set a pattern for him as we walked the road of everlasting life.

I love you, Son.
Dad

August 26, 1988

Dear Son,
This morning I am at the medical center with your mother. Soon, a new brother or sister of yours will enter this world, this life.

Is it not strange? One departs and another arrives. Only a season we spend on this stage. There is frightful brevity even in longevity, yet this is the way life is. Since whatever days we have must be spent, (I speak to myself also), let us spend them wisely and well.

With great affection,
Dad

PS Less than two hours ago, your sister arrived. I was present at the birth of each of my children, but this was different. I did not give birth, yet I feel so drained. I feel as if my emotions have been on a roller coaster. Your sister looks fine, and has such a calm personality. So far, so good!

Sept. 1, 1988

Dear Son,
When your great-grandfather's files were gone through, something turned up that I would like to share with you. A newspaper clipping from 1974 was found, a front page article from an art show I won at a very pivotal time in my life. The photo shows how I looked not long before my conversion. I must have looked something like that when I first entered the church doors.

May I tell you of my conversion? I was brought up not knowing God or even believing in His existence. So much of my time was filled with self-indulgence. I remember many days of my childhood, walking barefoot through mountains of garbage at the landfill.

Our home was wild and violent. We were heathen to the bone. I loved to party, loved my friends, loved my art and the recognition it brought. I loved pretty girls and had habits of drinking and smoking dope. My language was vulgar and profane. I have been a liar and a thief.

Early in life, I had friends among varied races, groups and communities. I often crossed boundaries and barriers just to have fun with my friends. My early successes as an artist inflated my ego greatly, and I became cocky.

But for all the enjoyment and thrill that seemed to be my obsession, there remained a profound emptiness in my heart. All the women I sought could not fill that void, neither could anything else.

When I was about 18 or 19, the mother of a friend of mine told me about Jesus, and salvation. That did not seem to be for me. The lifestyle I loved and the philosophy I had would not permit it. But she loved me and was patient.

After a while, I began to want to visit her church, but I was concerned about finding a pretext. What would my friends say, or rather, what would I say to them to account for my going to church? (Please don't allow your peers to control you.) Then a girl invited me. I had my excuse! I would say that I went with a girl.

The church was on the other side of the tracks, in a tough, hard area of town called Colonia. Colonia is nearly all Mexican and black, a real no man's land for white people.

At that church, culture shock. I had never seen anything like this. They lifted their hands and sang enthusiastically, and everyone in that church was black... except me.

The way I remember it, I laughed at, and in my mind made fun of some of the people at that church. Much more could be said, but I went back. It was like I was a fish and the Lord had a hook in my mouth. Eventually, the gospel found my heart.

Soon, I began to weigh things out, like on a scale. I was working during the summer as a forest firefighter, and as I worked on a mountain fire, I asked myself questions like, what would I trade for my soul?

If I was the best artist in the world, and lost my soul, what good would that be? Would I trade my soul for wealth, or recognition as a great artist? No.

I asked myself, would I trade my soul for any or all of the women I lusted for? No! Then I thought about my friends. If they loved me, they would be glad to see me get right with God.

I came to the conclusion that I had to get saved. I didn't know *how*, but I had to get saved. At once, I dropped all my girlfriends, stopped drinking and as I watched my dope flush down the toilet, I said to myself, "I must be serious about this." Ignorant as I was, I set my heart to seek the Lord.

The Lord did not hide from me. He saved me, changed me from the inside out. I'm just not the same. When He filled me with the Holy Ghost, I promised that I would never let Him go.

The world may never understand me, but I intend to keep my promise.

Love,
Dad

October 4, 1988

Dear Son,
How I love you. At this time you don't know about or understand the desperate financial struggles we are experiencing. The place where we have been staying is to be sold and we must leave very soon. We have little money.

When I come home with such a weight of responsibilities, imagine how refreshing it is to be greeted by you, so excited, so enthused. You tell me again and again how you love me. How rich I am! Your outpour of loving attention is like a wonderful medicine. It does my heart good.

I remember what it was like to be hungry. I remember how my stomach hurt. When you are older, please never forget what it was like to be poor. When you encounter someone less fortunate than you, don't allow yourself to despise that person.

Remember what it was like, and always treat him or her as you would want yourself to be treated. Be man enough to be sensitive and care. Don't forget.

With great affection,
Dad

PS Remember Tamar? (II Samuel 13) After her terrible experience she laid her hand on her head and went on crying. She remained desolate in her brother's house. She was shattered.

A person who is victimized does not have to remain a desolate, ongoing victim. God has something better. I know many people who are shattered, with lives that never seem to mend. They are like an open and untended wound, which carries infection and bitterness. God did not mean for our lives to be desolate, fruitless, empty or bitter.

Perhaps someone like you can tell the shattered person words that minister hope, giving both comfort and a reason to live on. Maybe you will bring the needed, soothing medicine. Never forget my son, what it is to be without, what is like to be cold. Some, in their days of comfort, have forgotten.

A person may be treated as worthless for so long, he or she may begin to think of their own value as equal to trash. When you see someone like that, always conduct yourself in a way that restores dignity, honor and worth, and reveals the great love that God has for them.

Remember, Son, that person is precious to God, and could be you or your son or daughter. That could be your mother or father. Don't let your heart grow cold.

October 21, 1988

Dear Son,
We now are not living where for the last 2 ½ years we called home. We had to get out. We are starting all over again in another city. There is strangeness in our lives, and things may get worse before they get better.

It's kind of scary for me, but I refuse to be intimidated. It seems like a march in a remote snowfall, where to quit is to die. What I have is hope. I believe that with the help of the Lord we can, and will, make it.

As a child, you are shielded from much of this. I suppose I would try to protect you from every unpleasantness, if I could. If only I could.

I would not trade you for all the money in the world. I wouldn't trade you for all the fish in the sea or all the rice in China. God has shared you with us and we are grateful. I have a verse for you, when you stand in my shoes. Psalm 56:3, "What time I am afraid, I will trust in thee."

Much love,
Dad

October 26, 1988

Dear Gershom,
Is it the light of morning that I see just ahead? Is it the glow that will chase away this long night? God is faithful, morning will come, and a new day will dawn.

I thought to say more, but I will end with this memory of Sunday. I visited this church, along with your mother, sister and brother. Though I was satisfied to come and listen, I was presented to the people to speak.

A wonderful thing happened as I preached. As I ministered God's Word to encourage and bless others, my soul was ministered to and greatly encouraged.

I was strengthened and blessed as I labored to strengthen and bless Christ's Church. Sometimes you have to encourage yourself in the Lord. What a mighty God we serve!

Love always,
Dad

These things I have spoken unto you, that in me ye might have peace. In the world ye shall have tribulation: but be of good cheer; I have overcome the world. John 16:33

November 11, 1988

Dear Gershom,

These days are somewhat difficult for you and your brother. What was so familiar is largely gone. However, we are all together, all healthy and strong.

We have much to give thanks for. Somehow I want to say things and do things that will have lasting impact. I desire that my art and my words and my deeds will benefit succeeding generations.

The sum of our passage through this world, this life, is but a few heartbeats and only a few days. You rise in the morning and meet the fullness of the day, only to find that the day declines, the night comes and you must rest.

Enjoy the day that God has given you and do well until you must sleep with your generation. If you are a wise man your sleep shall be sweet, very sweet.

Love,
Dad

November 12, 1988

Dear Son,
Today our family went to the beach. We took off our shoes and walked on the sand. We ran, we took our time, we had a good time.

It is very important to me to normalize our family life. I can see that so many recent things have profoundly affected your sense of security. So many changes of such great impact and the present distresses are affecting you. I can see it. I don't like it. I work to change this.

I am looking at you, now, as you sleep. What finer child could any man ask for? You, your brother and your sister demand great energies, but you all enrich my life.

I want to hold you as you are and behold the wonder of who you are. I am delighting in you as you are becoming all you shall be. Perhaps the privilege is so fleeting, I cannot savor it all. But I will try.

Love,
Dad

November 24, 1988
Thanksgiving Day
(about 12:30 AM)

Dear Son,
I think that the snoring I hear is yours. The family is asleep and now I have a little time and space to write. Earlier, I received a payment on a drawing and a down payment on a painting. We then were able to buy groceries and I bought your mother a pair of shoes. You boys and Anita went with us, and each boy received a small toy truck. I only had a penny prior to this. One penny.

About ten years ago, I worked for a man who resisted the gospel. This man had some expensive rings on his fingers. We were installing some drainpipes near some apartments. There were large sections of ivy bordering the buildings.

While I was working, he had mud on his hands, up to his wrists, and was trying to shake the mud off. As I worked a short distance away, I heard a high pitched ping, the sound of his ring as it bounced off the cement walk and then into a long stretch of ivy. I left what I was doing, and though I had not seen the area that it bounced into, I got on my knees in the ivy to help my boss find his ring.

Then the man made an odd statement to me. He said something to the effect that maybe God didn't want him to have the ring because it was too expensive. I suggested that perhaps that was not the reason, and then, with my eyes open and my mouth shut, I began to pray in the Spirit. I said, "Take the hand of thine anointed and let me find the ring." (I prayed in King James' language that day!)

Immediately, I thrust my hand directly into the ivy and pulled out the ring! Just like that. Then, I turned to the man, with my arm extended and the ring in hand, and said, "Just like you were concerned about this ring, God has been concerned about you!"

Your prayer life, Son, can set you up to be the right person, at the right place, at the right time, with the right stuff. Your prayer life can change the world. Take root downward and bear fruit upward, my son.

Love,
Dad

November 24, 1988
(Thanksgiving Day after dinner)

Dear Son,
When your mother carried you, I did not know you, what you would be like, what you would look like, but now I see you. Now I know you.

Isn't it like that in life? Some things will come. They are on their way, about to arrive on schedule. But in our living and waiting, we don't see them. In waiting, we may become anxious, angry and fretful.

Rest assured that God's timing is perfect. His way is always right, but almost never by the natural sight of our eyes are we to walk. We are called to walk by faith. God's train will arrive on time.

About twelve and a half years ago, after graduating from one college and needing to transfer to further my education, I left college. My father had lost his business and it did not seem to be right for me to continue my education as they lost everything. So I moved back home and worked a variety of jobs.

I washed dishes, painted homes, did gardening and menial tasks, whatever honest work I could find.

I cleaned toilets and did other things. I sometimes worked day and night to feed and house the family and myself. Sometimes they helped, sometimes and mostly, they did not.

While many of my peers were becoming doctors and lawyers, and I was the best artist of my peers, my hands were splitting open from work. It was socially embarrassing, but we survived, and I learned to pray.

After so many years, I moved on. I applied and was accepted at a university to finish my education. The financial aid form had a section my father needed to fill in, because I had lived at that address, but he would not fill it out.

To this day, I do not understand. I carried the man and his family, but my dad would not fill out part of a form. I could not go around it. It left me so bewildered and hurt, and shut out of the education I sought.

But education comes in many ways. I went to seminars and became autodidactic. I read books and diligently studied. I sought a good understanding, so I devoured the Word and gave myself to prayer and to serve others.

Waiting for God to move and respond to our prayers and tears can be such a long process, but don't give up. Don't quit. God will show Himself to the universe through us.

He will demonstrate His wisdom and power through our inadequacy and weakness. In the days you do not understand the storm or the cloud of your day, think on these words.

I love you. Trust Him always.
Dad

PS This was probably the last Thanksgiving that my mother will ever have in her father's house. We traveled to be with her and had a wonderful time.

February 2, 1989

Dear Son,
A wise son makes a glad father, and tonight I am glad. You are about 3 ½ years old and your brother is about 2 ½. While I was gone earlier, you both had church together. Josiah sang "In the Name of Jesus" and you preached. Your mother heard you quoting scriptures. Part of your text was Psalms 56:3 and 47:1.

Also, an older child was here waiting for her mother to get off of work. This little girl tried to get you to go into the bathroom were she was, but you had been taught better. You said, "That's not right." I am so delighted with you.

Earlier, when I was yet in bed, you took my reading light and put it by where my feet were and said, "Want a lamp unto your feet?"

A few days ago you had a temperature and your breathing was very strained. I don't remember ever seeing your breathing so difficult. We prayed and those symptoms are completely gone. God is so good to me.

Love,
Dad

March 29, 1989

Dear Son,

The strain is greatly lifted now. Our heads are a little above water. I was working three and four jobs because of our circumstances, our bills and debts. We have a place to live and I fully paid every penny of back rent from Alabama. The landlord was shocked.

A man should carry his own weight and pay what he owes. But I purposely cut back the pace because of what it was doing to me. I don't want to cause a stroke or heart attack. Since I slowed down my pace and cut back such demand on myself, we are eating, paying bills, you are wearing decent clothes and we are so happy as a family together.

When we first got this apartment, we kept our food in a bucket with ice. One day I left for work, and when I came back that night, our apartment was fully furnished! I can look back in wonder at how abundantly God has blessed us through a crisis. I want to be what you need me to be, and I'm trying.

Love,
Dad

May 1, 1989

Dear Son,
I got off work about 2 hours ago. My body feels like a rusty machine. All of you are sleeping now. It is well with us.

I want to encourage you to be real. No one else is you. You are special. Avoid the pitfall of the proud, who proposed to build a tower, saying, "Let us make us a name."

There are some that have built themselves a tower and sat upon a throne, yet God was forced to oppose them. Why? God resists the proud.

So be sincere, avoid the pitfall and walk humbly with the Lord.

With great affection,
Dad

PS Remember that in God's eyes the greatest one is the servant of all. What of it if your name is not trumpeted before men? God sees! He rewards far better!

May 4, 1989

Dear Son,

It is important for us to maintain our focus and to minister life. The flesh adds nothing to God. The Spirit gives life.

When a religious organization becomes, in effect, a spiritual abortion clinic, I am convinced that God will have His babes birthed and nourished elsewhere, somewhere safer.

It is of utmost importance for you to maintain the integrity of your walk with the Lord, regardless of what other men do. Keep those eyes on Jesus, Son. People will get you off the track, if you let them.

Love,
Dad

May 7, 1989

Dear Son,

Some time ago, I was at the house I grew up in. The house was run down, the exterior overgrown. It looks like an illustration to the words, "And sin when it is finished brings death."

I have some fond memories of happier times there, but they are heavily outweighed and overshadowed by the dark clouds of very painful memories and unhappy times.

I was distinctly called by God to "come out from among them." This is what I have done.

(At this point, my drowsiness is demanding that I come to a conclusion. It is, again, quite late.)

Love,
Dad

May 20, 1989

Dear Son,
Your mother and I have celebrated another anniversary. (Where did the time go?) I appreciate your mother more and more. You are like an arrow I take to the bow, point to the target and let fly. Your life and success in the will of God is enormously important to me. Avoid strange women.

There are women whose words are sweet and whose end is bitter. Leave such women alone. The adulteress will hunt for you like a predator and you must remember, son, you are not fireproof. The word of God says "flee" and you must not linger.

As a single young man, I saw a moth nearly escape an open flame. It returned again and again until, poof! No more moth. I observed this and took heed to my ways.

This world invites us strongly into its adultery. But there are some things, once set in motion, you can be utterly powerless to stop, and you cannot undo. A lifetime of regret can be yours. Shame can be your shadow.

A far happier course can be found in God's wife for you and God's will for you.

A wise man can be happier longer than a fool. Remember, my son, it is the pure in heart who shall see God. I long to see you in that day.

Love,
Dad

PS Your own heart may betray you, but the Lord will help you. Trust Him.

May 21, 1989

Dear Son,
Your mother had a dream not long ago. In it, she and I were walking among some ruins, and now and then we would see someone wandering among the ruins. Whenever we saw someone, in this dream, she would hear a song that said, "We're so tired of being lost and we don't have any place to call home."

Whenever a religious movement departs from Christ and becomes a kingdom of men, of demons or whatever, it will not stand. It must fall. What a waste it would be to pour one's life's energies into meaningless religious exercises and become as dumb, sterile cattle led about by some blind profiteer.

The gospel is the power of God unto salvation. Jesus yet saves. His power to deliver is not weakened by the darkness of the day. Meaningful life is found in Him.

If the church or movement departs from Christ, I say, stay with Christ. You won't ever have to sing that song, "We're so tired of being lost and we don't have any place to call home."

If you stay with Jesus and with his Word, you won't be lost and you will have a home. I want to see you there.

Love,
Dad

June 30, 1989
(about midnight)

Dear Son,
Today my heart was enriched. The Lord revealed to me a wonderful thing.

It began as I remembered what I prayed for as a young believer. The desire of my heart, the cry of my heart had been that I might know Him, as Paul wrote, in Philippians 3:10, "That I may know Him, and the power of His resurrection, and the fellowship of His sufferings, being made conformable unto His death."

In many things and over years, I have suffered injustice, humiliation and pain. But today, it was like a curtain was pulled back, allowing me to see through the window. I began to see how these things that hurt so very much, have been the means of God granting me that which I asked.

Through those things I suffered, though I had been a believer, I now know Jesus Christ in a fuller dimension. Through those things, I know Jesus in the fellowship of His suffering. Through those devices, He somehow brought life out of what was killing me.

I appreciate the great wisdom of God, His kindness and faithfulness. I did not see His loving hand in these things as I do now.

I am a man so greatly blessed.

Love,
Dad

PS A certain man, a high church official, who has greatly harmed me, may never humble himself and repent for what he has done. I confess that I told this man, that if he wanted to cheat me, to "Go ahead and cheat me. God is going to judge between you and me."

The transaction of forgiveness is imperfect except the offender turn from his actions, then to ask for and receive forgiveness. Nevertheless, my forgiveness will remain available to him. I pray that God forgives him also.

It is time to go forward and not dwell on the hurts of the past. Those things we put behind us, and we escape the prison of a bitter heart. The truth is what we are concerned with, and it is the truth that keeps us free.

July 11, 1989

Beloved Son,
It is good to have a vision. It is good to be able to look ahead beyond your obstacles, to see a new and better future, to see far beyond every season, every misery and every dead-end.

It is good to have, not a wishy-washy, any-way-the-wind-blows kind of existence, but to have certain expectations, based on certain promises. A godly vision is a great treasure.

For quite some time, I have wanted to write to you about death, but not now. Perhaps soon.

I am about finished with a painting of you and your brother Josiah, I have been working on since March. I am thinking of titling it "Brothers and Best Friends," though I originally thought to call it "Two Mixed-Race Boys." Perhaps it will be marketable in reproductions. I kind of like it. I certainly like you.

Love,
Dad

August 3, 1989

Dear Son,
Tonight your words indicated something of a child's perspective. They sounded poetic. You felt my arm and told me, with music and wonder in your voice, "Daddy, you are very strong, and high as the sun. Let me see you touch the sun."

You children are a high priority to me, and having cut back on other things, I am investing much of my life in you. The days of the week slip through my fingers like so many loose pearls.

You're a beautiful boy and I think you will become a good and wonderful man.

Love,
Dad

August 16, 1989

Dear Gershom,

Recently I have chastised you for lying to me. One day, you seemed to be so apprehensive of receiving a spanking concerning a certain deed, that you lied to me. Not long after, you lied to me again.

After I spoke with you, and you tried so hard to persuade me otherwise, I spanked you.

A day or so later, I asked you about another certain deed. When you admitted responsibility, I commended you for telling me the truth. You risked the possibility of punishment for the deed in order to tell me the truth. That is progress.

Love,
Dad

PS Tonight you told me that you didn't want to be "selfish," but a "nice fish." Ha. Let me see you touch the sun, Gershom.

September 7, 1989

Dear Son,
I must make important decisions, seeking God's guidance. But now, there is so much I do not see. I hate indecisiveness, but it is wise to wait on the voice of the Lord.

I have thought of an arrow that is kept hidden in a quiver. At just the right moment, the archer reaches for his arrow, takes perfect aim as he draws it back on the string, and lets it fly to the mark.

I am an arrow in the quiver. An arrow is powerless to project itself, unable to find the proper mark on its own. It seems so foolish and weak, doesn't it? Ah yes, foolish and weak, except for the Bowman, who with perfect knowledge, perfect timing and perfect aim, sets it to flight toward the appointed mark. I am an arrow in the quiver of God, hidden there.

Do you have questions of life also? Are your decisions tough and heavy, also? God's perfect will for you is available, but only attained if you make yourself available to Him.

The divine Bowman always finds His mark. Just believe and let Him have His way.

I love you, my son,
Dad

September 14, 1989

Dear Son,
It is amazing how blessed we are. It is amazing also how dull my thinking, and how my heart is so void of thanksgiving, at times.

Shortly before I went to work, I was doing some volunteer counseling as an aide to the chaplain at the California Youth Authority.

One young man I spoke with had such a profoundly painful existence. His mother is Vietnamese and his father is African American. The Vietnamese people do not accept, or rather, they reject him because of his father's color and nationality. His father is in another state.

This young man is eighteen years, and I observe him looking down, seldom, if ever, making eye contact. His victimization continues even in his confinement.

He professes to be a Christian, and I hope to God that he is. In time, I will fan that small flicker of life into a flame, if I can. I will be his friend and build him up and build into his life.

Frank E. Robinson, Jr.

In the short time we shared, I told him that he was like a rose bud, surrounded by thorns, and given the right amount of sunshine and water, would blossom and become beautiful.

I thank God for my wife and beautiful children. We have so much.

I love you,
Dad

September 29, 1989

Dear Son,
Someone gave me a Bible when I was about 19 years of age. I think it was a while before I started reading it. But when I began, and my appetite grew, it was, and has been, such a rich, marvelous experience.

The day that I lived in said, "There are no absolutes." It was a day of self-indulgence, of, "Do your own thing" and "If it feels good do it." I bought into that for a season, yet my heart was in conflict.

Ah, but those words! Those golden words brought light into my soul! God's Word gives life. I read the New Testament straight through. Then I began to read more. I read as one attempting to make up for lost time, as a hungry man. My life began to conform to the great truths I was learning.

God doesn't change. His character is not altered whether we are with or against Him. He doesn't vacillate like a politician that jockeys for approval. God is not dependent on us.

If our history colors facts or simply ignores Him, and if science exalts itself (as if true science could possibly exist without Him), God is not moved or shaken. The world lied.

Are you ready for an absolute? How about this? God is. He exists. Here is another: God rewards people who seek Him diligently.

(It's after 2 AM now, I must close.)

I love you,
Dad

Thy words were found, and I did eat them: and thy word was unto me the joy and rejoicing of mine heart: for I am called by thy name, O Lord God of hosts.
Jeremiah 15:15

October 1, 1989

Dear Son,
I just finished looking at a large book by John Singer Sargent's art. The work was so marvelous. His work was brilliant, skillful, great.

Within my heart is the knowledge, or perhaps merely the conviction, that that caliber of art is not unreachably above or beyond grasp in this life. Also within me is the frustration this sometimes produces.

How is it that I would ever fully develop, explore and expand upon this gift God gave to me, unless I was committed to drawing and painting exclusive of almost everything else? Perhaps there is a balance in the will of God somewhere, yet I have not figured it out. I am pulled in many competing directions.

I try to give the greater time and weight to things of eternal consequence, yet achievement in the world of art seems to demand at least a full time effort.

For me, my art can only find spurts of time, here and there. It is like an unfulfilled promise. But I am uncomfortable with the posture of shrugging shoulders and giving up to mediocrity because God has called me to preach and serve.

Your dilemmas may be different, but I trust God to fill the empty hands that reach for Him, with the gift of understanding and the knowledge of His will.

Love,
Dad

October 2, 1989
(about 1:10AM)

Dear Son,
Earlier, we got ready to go to church, got everyone outside, locked the door and discovered that my keys were missing. After we got back inside and searched my keys were finally found in the toy box.

We got to church in time to hear the minister teach. He spoke about Abraham offering Isaac and God's provision.

Talk about hitting the nail on the head! Even so, I still have incomplete knowledge as to the will of God concerning my art, ministry and other aspects of life, but I am willing to yield to Him whatever He desires.

I love you, Son,
Dad

October 10, 1989
(after midnight)

Dear Son,
A few weeks ago I took you to an abortion clinic protest. Usually the method of protesting by picket line, etc. is not my style. I prefer praying and seeking God to bring about a change, but in this case I made an exception.

Abortion is apparently very lucrative. It is moral insanity. It is defined as a woman's right. It is unnatural for a mother to pay someone to dismember or otherwise destroy her unborn offspring. Barbaric. At this point, our law still permits it.

The absurdity is that those who would protect that helpless unborn child are made to look the part of barbarian and fanatic.

It is just like the devil to make good look obscene, and make obscenity look good. It's like the world to swallow what the devil says. Thank God this world is not our home.

Love,
Dad

PS I stopped by my Dad's after work. He had been drinking and was so argumentative that I left abruptly. Part of me feels like never seeing him again, yet that doesn't seem right, so I probably will see him again. I will continue to pray for him. It is far easier to burn a bridge than to build one.

October 11, 1989

Dear Son,

Soon these writings to you will be less frequent. I want to invest a similar quality of time and thought into a collection of letters to your brother, and then to your younger sister. Further, I would like to write short inspirational booklets. It seems there is no end to the list of things I would like to accomplish.

One day I would like to sit, with your children playing on my knees and at my feet. It seems that it would be a most enjoyable thing.

It was almost a year ago that we were, in effect, homeless. We started over with almost nothing. We borrowed a room for two months and I found work, sought more work and we prayed. I worked three and four jobs and it was very demanding.

On the precise date of two months, we were approved for our present apartment and had the money. I remind you sometimes of that time of praying. We now see and enjoy what God's hand has provided. We didn't see it then, but we believed and hoped and waited and worked.

I think it is safe to agree with the psalmist who said, "It is a good thing to give thanks unto the Lord…." Know what? I really love you and I always will. You are my boy and I'm not ashamed of you at all.

Give it your best, Son.

Love,
Dad

October 14, 1989

Dear Son,
You know, for the past several years I have experienced much. It seems like for so many years I've been in school, God's school.

I have suffered more than some, but far less than others. In a sense, I would not trade the worst events or greatest periods of pain. Why? Because through them I have acquired things otherwise unavailable.

I know the Lord more intimately, more deeply, having tasted the pain of my cross and the joy of His life and power. Those words roll out so easily, but they were not so easy to live.

When God brings strangers my way, (perhaps some came by way of the devil), and I am privileged to be an ambassador of Jesus Christ, and share the love of God with them, the thrill of that experience is like an addictive narcotic for me. It's a clean, holy thrill, and then I want it again.

Why would God want to use me? I was the one who was so low down. I was an ignorant heathen, self-centered, dirty and sometimes a violent young man.

It nearly boggles my mind to have a glimpse, a fleet glance revealed of God's thinking concerning me. And to think, it isn't even over yet.

Have you ever thought about how or what God thinks about you? Before the world was made, He had you in His thoughts. It nearly boggles the mind.

I love you,
Dad

October 17, 1989

Dear Son,

It is really something to consider that Moses treasured and esteemed the reproach of Christ greater riches than Egypt's treasure. His eyes were fixed on the ultimate reward.

When he first left Egypt after killing an Egyptian, his choice of identity had been made. He forfeited access to an earthly throne for access to a greater, heavenly throne.

Even so, there was a space of many years. We find that Moses kept the flock of Jethro. This was an abomination according to the culture of Egypt he had known and was trained in. If Moses' former peers could have seen him then, his estate would be noted as disgraceful. Could this at least be part of the process God used to bring Moses to the place where he was the meekest of all men?

I heard a story. I want you to imagine three ugly women who lived in a remote country. One day the prince of that country rode through their village and they were given papers, signed by the prince himself, granting them authority to enter the royal city.

As the three hurried to this great invitation, it was observed that their very appearance was changed. They had become beautiful. Even though the city seemed so far away, it was only a few days later that they entered through the royal gates.

One of the women was content just to enter the city, but the other two went on to the castle. Upon entering the prince's castle the one woman said to the other, "I am content. What more could anyone want? I am now in the very castle of the prince."

Her friend looked this way and that way and replied, "It is a blessing to make it to the city, and an honor to be in the castle of the prince, but since that day in our old village, I have loved the prince, and I will only be content when I am with him," and she went on.

What difference does it make if everyone or anyone approves of you and understands you? Keep your eyes fixed on the ultimate reward. Go after it. Win the prize.

Love,
Dad

December 31, 1989

Dear Son,
This writing is in the last hour of the 1980's. All of us are in our beds and it is very well with us.

We recently had the best Christmas our family has experienced. This is such a wonderful time for me. It blessed me so to see my children happy and enjoying life. Just look where God has brought us from. My soul humbly gives Him thanks.

My heart mirrors those words of David. *I had fainted, unless I had believed to see the goodness of the Lord in the land of the living. Wait on the Lord: be of good courage, and he shall strengthen thine heart: wait, I say, on the Lord.* Psalms 27:13, 14

Wait, I say on the Lord. Don't faint, it will pay off after a while.

Love,
Dad

~ Hello, 1990.

January 1, 1990

Dear Son,
Yesterday you let me know how big I am in your eyes. You told me that no one is as big as I am.

You also shared with me something I didn't know. You are intimidated about starting kindergarten. That is understandable. You expressed that you want me to go with you, and that you want to escape to a place that has rides you can go on.

I think I can help you to climb this mountain. Maybe some of it we can climb together. One truth we are trying to build into your life is that, even if we can't go with you everywhere, the Lord will.

Everything is going to be all right.

Love,
Dad

January 5, 1990

Dear Son,
This morning you climbed on my bed and gave me a hug. You said, "God gave you to me."

I have no words adequate to describe the richness of that moment.

A man with a great treasure am I.

Love,
Dad

February 2, 1990

Dear Son,
You are a very articulate person. I understand that you spoke very straightforwardly to your grandfather about his smoking a few days ago. This, and more at the age of four.

Last Saturday, after you discovered a bird dropping on your shirt, you remarked that the bird didn't even come back to say he was sorry.

Then again you made up a song that went something like this:
"Fire, fire, fire.
Devil's gonna be in the fire
He wants to be up high
But God's gonna put him in the fire
Liar, liar, liar.
All the liars gonna be in the fire."

Your brother, Josiah, now three, responded to your song by making his voice deep and singing something like: "God don't like the bad things that the devil do." Your mother asked you where you learned that song. You said, "I learned it in my heart."

These moments and days, once again, are like beads or pearls that slip through my fingers to the ground. When we are gone, and the wind passes over the places we have stood and walked, what will remain of what we have done? What will have weight and value? What will eternity reveal? Questions to consider, my articulate son.

Love,
Dad

February 18, 1990

Dear Son,
The fireplace is down to embers and it is late. I've finalized notes for a speaking engagement and all of you are asleep.

I have contentment. I'm satisfied. I'm rich.

Love,
Dad

Frank E. Robinson, Jr.

February 25, 1990

Dear Son,

At four years of age, you make up and sing songs. It gives me such delight and satisfaction to hear you do this. You are my boy.

A few hours ago, as you were bathing, you talked about becoming big, like me, and to have a mustache like I have, and also to have hair like mine. Yours is very curly and my hair is straight.

It is interesting and entertaining to observe you.

Love,
Dad

March 2, 1990

Dear Son,
Several hours ago, before I went to work, a former minister spoke with me. He has a drug problem. This man knows right from wrong, but willfully chooses the destructive course.

He asked me to preach at his funeral. I am unable to persuade him, it seems. It depresses me and breaks my heart.

What is it that a man craves at all costs? What is it that exacts death from a man, through he has offered his wife, children and job, his future and his present?

Perhaps increasingly close encounters with death are addictive intoxicants. It's a giddy game of Russian roulette. I will continue to pray. I don't know what else to do.

Love,
Dad

March 23, 1990

Dear Son,
Yesterday I spoke with a very successful man. He wants me on his staff at a large church in Los Angeles. The salary is more than I have made in my life. The opportunity for professional refinement and exposure is great.

I appreciate the kindness of God and His tender consideration of us. Isn't He wonderful?

Love,
Dad

PS I feel like the smoke is clearing and everyone can see I'm standing on a rock. He brought me out of the miry clay and put my feet on the rock to stay.

April 22, 1990

Dear Son,
It feels like a chapter is closing and another is about to begin. The church board voted unanimously in my favor regarding my employment in Los Angeles.

My mind has many ideas for progress in various areas of ministry. However, wisdom dictates that I close my mouth, open my ears, grasp what my new duties will be, and master them. Then, as God opens doors for me, I intend to share my ideas.

Also, I am very concerned about the direction the local church that I started at is going. It is not in my hands to fix, and now I am to leave the area. Therefore, I have given them up to God. Perhaps one day He will send me back to help them.

Our future is bright, because we trust Him.

Love,
Dad

June 11, 1990

Dear Son,
Today you are five years of age. Our family went to the zoo, returned and had cake. You opened gifts.

I have been working long hours, making our time together as a family more precious.

The present experiences for me are educational. I suppose that in the purpose of God, so much is hidden, that I cannot see now, but will be of benefit later. I will trust Him with my present and future.

Five years, my son, ran ever so swiftly. It has been a great adventure, eh?

I am praying for you.

Love,
Dad

June 19, 1990

Dear Son,
It is more important to me to be right (not self-righteous) than to be rich.

Truth is a shield for us. Let us stand where there is strong light. Because we love God and embrace His Son, we hate evil continually.

Our culture changes rapidly. Decades pass and walls crumble. We have been born into a kingdom in which the King is, and shall forever be, a non-changer.

How can we represent Him?

By Him we are enabled. He chose me, transformed me, therefore I am what He has made me to be. He made our assignment and He enables us to do it.

Only by His power and Spirit are we able to represent a living God to a world of dead men.

Love,
Dad

PS A man assessed my current employment and said there are men who would leave wife and kids to be in my shoes. I said "That's the difference between me and them. I would not leave my wife and kids to be in my shoes."

July 9, 1990

Dear Son,
How precious is your identity? Can we really find a place within us totally and irrevocably given to God?

If it is possible to live a life dead to our selfish will and alive to the will of God, is not a change of identity a reasonable and normal prerequisite or consequence?

I mull over your future, and ask, who will you serve? How will you be identified? To what will you surrender your heart? In my heart I believe that you will love God with all sincerity and with understanding.

I thank God for you, my boy. Might as well not worry about what mere men think about you.

I will always love you.

Always,
Dad

July 12, 1990

Dear Son,

I was working on a floral arrangement today, and a saying came to mind. I would like to share it with you: "A competitor is not necessarily an enemy. A competitor brings out the best in you."

I don't think we would know how great a boxer Muhammad Ali was without Joe Frazier. So, recognize who your competitor is and appreciate him. Identify your enemy and love him.

If you bow down, God will lift you up. Just wait and you will see. It will work out just fine.

Love,
Dad

July 14, 1990

Dear Son,
Church growth is hindered by an unwillingness to change or adapt.

Some may say, "God doesn't change. Our methods worked for us and we do not need to change." This argument may be dearly held, but it is flawed reasoning. Because, while it is true that God and His message do not change, our culture constantly and rapidly does change.

We are not called to enshrine yesterday's methods. We are called to evangelize and affect the generation in which we exist. If our methods and strategies are not working, let us find new strategies and methods.

Notice the natural growth of a plant from a seed to maturity. Change is natural as it grows and matures, from stage to stage. Notice that this change is not in its essence or substance. Corn is corn, whether the mere kernel or mature stalk, and it is corn through every stage in between.

We should not fear, when God trims away dead religious trappings, either in us or around us.

He is known to do this as part of healthy and fruitful spiritual growth.

We should not criticize or injure ministries that are not status quo, or just don't fit into narrow-minded definitions. Get a broader view.

If God chooses and anoints someone, who are we to say He can't? Discern by asking, is the essence Christ? Is the substance Christ? The message? And what is the fruit?

I think most of the prophets, and many of the saints who were murdered, arrived on the scene in a generation that loved their own dead trappings.

Actively resist and expose the dead stuff of your day, or it may be an indicator that you are blind and spiritually dead along with them.

If, however, you are alive to God and you see clearly (I trust that this will be the case), only allow yourself to be their reprover if you have prepared yourself to die. A coward's life is not life.

Love,
Dad

PS Several hours ago, I spoke with my grandfather's

only living sister, Auntie Winifred. She told me that her mother was a Christian. One day, this woman (my great-grand mother) went to a house of prostitution on a soul winning venture. If I understand the story correctly, she converted the Madame! Isn't that great? That's a point of my ancestry I did not know, but I certainly appreciated hearing about it.

July 18, 1990

Dear Son,
Again my thoughts address identity.

There is a proper place for self-defense. A good name, for example, is worth protecting. But some ego needs are overvalued, too fragile, held too tightly. Your image may become your idol. Something in me says to let it go, let it break if need be, let it go.

Who are you? What are you?

I am what God has called me to be. I am who He has made me to be and I have what He has given to me. My definition involves Him. Another person's labeling of you or me may or may not be accurate. So what? I know who I am.

Who are you, my son, do you know? Is your image so precious to you that you cannot trust God with it? Let it go, let it break, let it go.

Love,
Dad

July 24, 1990

Dear Son,
Later this morning I am to attend a funeral of a young woman who was killed on the same day that she brought her child to be dedicated to the Lord. It is very sad.

A man made a statement to me, to the effect that I love to help black people. That sounds so patronizing doesn't it? I perceive that I am misunderstood.

I drink from a cup that makes a person's racial or national heritage dissolve into a non-issue. I love people. I hate wrongdoing. I hate evil, and in the gospel, I have a transcendent cure for our wretched disease.

I am not certain how others use the term, "my people." Perhaps in reference to race, religion or nation, this term is used. "My people," who are my people?

A black man can observe acts wrongly committed upon others of his race and identify with them. In this context, "my people" would be understood.

To contrast with that, let's say that the wrong doer is a white man. I observe that, and as far as I can remember, never thought, "My people," in reference to him.

Somehow God made men, all of one blood, yet with variety in size, shape, and color. Beyond that, language and cultures vary so greatly.

Who are my people? The people who love God and follow Him, they are my people. Have I lost my identity? Quite frankly, yes. It was buried with Jesus. Am I without identity? No. He gave me a new one when He rose in my heart. I am now a son of God.

This is the cup that I drink from. I see people differently than some. I love to help all people. I would like to share this cup with you. Come and drink with me.

Love,
Dad

August 13, 1990

Dear Son,
I am the beneficiary of such kindness during this chapter of my sojourn on earth. I am so grateful to God.

Last night I preached at one of the largest churches in Los Angeles. I talked about being imprisoned by the bruises and abuse of yesterday and the fact that Jesus came to set us free.

Afterwards, I received good feedback. It was as if I had used a can opener to get past a well-protected place. The Word found some hearts.

This gives me immense happiness and satisfaction. This is who I am.

Love,
Dad

August 20, 1990

Dear Son,

I have sent the family to Alabama for your Auntie Marilyn's wedding and for a vacation. It is good to protect family ties, if possible. You are all to return day after tomorrow by train.

Last Saturday, for the first time in perhaps ten or more years, my family of origin was in the same place at the same time. It was somewhat awkward and strange.

I would say more, but not now. Let it suffice to say that my parents and their children have been disjointed and polarized. It has generated pain and anguish. God knows.

Perhaps that will help you to understand why my wife and you children are to me, Manasseh. As Joseph said, for God has made me forget all my toil, and all my father's house. Amen. I look forward to the arrival of your train.

Love,
Dad

August 22, 1990

Dear Son,
In a number of cases church leadership has been passed from father to son, much like a monarchy, or a Mom and Pop business. Sometimes this is good, other times, disastrous.

Biblical examples are plentiful. Observe Eli and his sons, also Samuel and his sons. Various others demonstrate very godly men, fathering wicked sons, and bad men that father righteous sons. A son advanced, but unworthy, probably knows this in his heart of hearts. His resulting insecurity is therefore understandable.

Let someone anointed come to his church, and it may cause him to feel threatened. The ears of true sheep will hear and they will respond, but the man's kingdom suffers exposure by way of contrast and plain truth.

Do not settle for a second hand, second rate, so-called ministry. Rather, open your hands to God and let Him equip you. Open your eyes, and let Him show you. Open your ears and your heart, He will teach you and fill you.

A second-hand anointing is no anointing at all. You must receive from God. Of course, you may stir and excite and challenge without true spiritual power. But true power will demonstrate itself in transformed lives. Do changed lives follow in your wake?

Don't settle simply for what I can give to you. I can't give you that much, anyway. Reach past me to God for yourself. He will bring you forward to the cutting edge, and to a place only His sons and daughters may go.

Love,
Dad

September 5, 1990

Dear Son,
A few hours ago I viewed the scene of a fatal shooting. The man had been killed earlier in the day.

A man pointed out to me what was apparently the residual stain of blood on the ground. It wasn't heavy and dark, but more faint, as if an attempt had been made to wash it away.

I looked and contemplated. I haven't his name, haven't seen his face (as far as I know), but I saw evidence of his life. There was the life of some woman's son, spilled out.

Was this man a father? What was his age? God knows. People will walk over that spot, and go about life's business, not aware that a man lost his life there.

A vapor, this life. Spend well.

Love,
Dad

September 10, 1990

Dear Son,
In the morning, we shall arise to your first day of school. This is a milestone, a first for us.

Your eyes are clear, beautiful and intelligent. You have a great deal of energy. We have worked with you and built into you, that you might be secure. The school is only a block or so away, but a big step, this kindergarten.

May God keep you and protect you, cause you to be fruitful and blessed, cause you to be a blessing in this world and an inheritor of that which is to come.

You are my son, and I love you so much.

Truly,
Dad

September 14, 1990

Dear Son,
Begin to practice hearing. Listen before responding. We jump to conclusions, and too often, the behavior of others is misinterpreted, based only on reflex assessments.

God gave me very quick reflexes, but they must not emerge from their proper place to overrule reason, wisdom and judgment. Give the other person space. Give that person the benefit of the doubt. Perhaps there are unseen, unknown factors involved.

Here's another thing, give people some rope and observe what they do with it. Let them talk. Let them talk some more. They may verbally hang themselves.

Become the person who is secure enough to wait, to listen and to discern. Deal with truth apart from emotions, especially anger or revenge. Safety is of the Lord and you are of the Lord.

Love,
Dad

PS Assumptions are not always valid, often wrong. Sometimes you just don't know. Keep your eyes open and your heart listening.

September 17, 1990

Dear Son,
Very early in the morning a call came in, a dear friend had died. This was my comrade in Alabama, an intellectual, articulate, big and tough man. I had built into his life and was enriched in exchange, as iron that sharpens iron. My heart is broken.

Put my tears into your bottle, O God, they are written in your book, are they not?

Perhaps I will write more later, I am very tired.

Love,
Dad

September 17, 1990

Dear Son,
This morning your sister Anita got ahold of this book again. She had scribbled over some part of this book. Suffice it to say that I am not highly pleased with such behavior, but I still like her. In fact, I still love her.

Please let me tell you more about my friend that died. In January 1984, when I first ran a revival meeting in Brewton, Alabama, Brother Rick came to hear me preach.

Later, when I had moved to Alabama, I ran a vacation Bible School. Brother Rick helped by driving many of our students. He was Baptist, and wanted a VBS at their church, way out in the country. He wanted me to help him and I consented. Our success in these projects, and the impact they had, helped to open doors for me there. He was a Baptist preacher.

On one occasion, I spoke at that Baptist church out in the woods. They were very traditional, generationally religious. The message that day was "The Religious Rebel," from Isaiah 1. The Holy Ghost brought such a shaking of the slumbering and dead spirits there. The place was like a beehive, afterward.

I was the only white person there and probably the only one for miles. I was confronted after church and was unsure about the probability of leaving before being beaten. My thinking was that if I get beat, then I just get beat. I had told the truth. Later that night, an apology was sent to me from the man who confronted me. It was Brother Rick who told me that the other man apologized for his actions.

I loved Brother Rick. He left the Masonic Lodge in response to the scripture. He even left the Baptist church and became a Holiness preacher. When I was taking your mother across the state line for your birth, I stopped the car on the way and spoke briefly to Brother Rick. Your mother may still be upset with me about that!

In 1987, after almost two years of not seeing Brother Rick, I returned to Alabama and we walked down a railroad track together, talking. Time ran away. You were someone special to him. Last month, when I sent you to Alabama, he got to see you. When he saw you, he could think of many fond memories.

Yesterday, after I got the news of his death, I walked through a side door of the church. A magnificent praise was filling the building. "He has made me glad, He has made me glad, I will rejoice for He has made me glad…I will enter His gates with thanksgiving in my heart and enter his courts with praise." The song went on.

I closed my eyes, envisioning Brother Rick, in the presence of God, approaching Him in the presence of such praise. He has made me glad He has made me glad, I will rejoice for He has made me glad.

I wept until I needed to step out the door to regain my composure. His wife lost a husband, his mother lost a son, I have lost a friend.

Love,
Dad

September 23, 1990

Dear Son,
By no means let me masquerade in your mind as perfect, I am not.

Yesterday, I rented a video of the cartoon "Peter Pan." After you and the other children saw the film, a neighbor child was seen looking in the window of our apartment. In response to her discovery, you boys leaped on the couch, and I saw you on the inside of the curtain as if you'd fallen down.

I raised my voice at you. It got immediate results. But, afterwards, I thought of a couple of things that made me feel that my reaction was too harsh.

First, you had just seen a lively, leaping, flying children's adventure. You needed an outlet for your excitement. You needed some running around, jumping and leaping space.

Secondly, I do not know the circumstances that bought that little girl to our window. Whatever the circumstances, I don't feel that the edge of my raised voice was a good example of Christ's love expressed in our home. I felt guilty on two counts.

Frank E. Robinson, Jr.

The home should radiate within and without the love of God, sacrificial, full of grace and mercy. Practically, my failures are noted, and I am so dependent upon God's grace and forgiveness.

When you become a parent, please reflect upon these words. Personally, Son, I think that you will be a good father and a good husband to your bride.

God will help you if you desire.

Love,
Dad

November 11, 1990

Dear Son,
There is a part of me that generally is not seen by my superiors in ministry. I practice meekness, deference and servanthood, especially esteeming them in a place of respect.

There are times and places that God gives me an incredible, Holy Ghost boldness. Once, I was in the "wrong place" for a white man, late at night. There were a number of teenagers around in the streets, but the Spirit of God rose up in me, and, in a sense, I took over.

In this setting, I began to lead one young man in the sinner's prayer. While we were praying, another fellow intruded, practically driving his motor bike between us and then he stopped. Seems like I didn't miss a beat. I straightly asked him, "Do you want to be saved?"

I had control and put him on the spot. He looked at me and answered "Yes." I told him to get off the bike. He got off and joined the other fellow in repentance and asked Jesus into his life.

There are a number of other wonderful events, but I do not mean to be proud or boast.

It is my understanding that servanthood is desired of me by God. Therefore I endeavor to conduct myself accordingly.

Do you wish to be a servant? You will be amazed at the ways God will use you to express Himself. It will be beyond you.

Don't fall into the trap of needing to be noticed by others. Just quietly do what the Lord asks. If nobody knows, it is well known in Heaven. The rewards and recognition God gives greatly exceed the laurels of men, that wither so quickly.

Love,
Dad

December 4, 1990

Dear Son,
A couple of my writings are being published around this date. A few are to be published later this month.

Part of my purpose, at this juncture of life, is to germinate the thinking of some people God will bring forward tomorrow. This is my belief. I am too exhausted right now to go into much detail, but the next few months should be interesting.

I love you, my boy,
Dad

January 1, 1991

Dear Son,
Tonight you asked if one of us in the family is white. I told you, "Yes." You then asked me, "Who is it?"

I was praying inside my heart, and instead of directly speaking to you, I had your mother come and sit next to me. You looked at us for a while, first one, then the other, back and forth, and then declared, "Oh, you're the one!" Those are more or less your precise words.

These are exciting days for me. I am working to develop an interracial ministry within the context of a large predominantly African-American, urban church. I am in opposition to the gospel of isolation. This is a challenging day. Your innocence is refreshing.

Love,
Dad

PS At five years old, you also wanted to know why husband and wife got to sleep in the master bedrooms, and not husband and their sons. Hmmm… such an inquisitive mind!

January 4, 1991

Dear Gershom,
In about 24 hours we may, as a country, be at war with the nation of Iraq. Many will die, in all probability. If we do not go to war at this time, it may very well be that many more people will be killed in a more devastating conflict later.

God help us all.

Love,
Dad

January 15, 1991

Dear Son,

Not long ago, I went in and looked at you children as you slept. You scarcely knew that I was there.

I thought about how it can be so similar with our Heavenly Father and us. He watches over us, and in our slumbering state, we may be so unaware of His affection and His sentiments of love toward us.

I looked, tonight, at Anita's hair and I noticed her mouth. I observed her embracing her doll as she slept. You were only partially under your blanket, and Josiah had a different pillow tonight.

If I observe you and if I'm involved with your life, even when you are not aware of it, should we think of our Heavenly Father's intimate observation of us and involvement with us as any less? Of course not.

We can rest in His love toward us.

Love,
Dad

February 2, 1991

Dear Son,
Earlier tonight, you told me that I am the best dad in the world.

I swam upstream, like a salmon, and rowed hard against the tide so long. But for a moment it is still, calm and peaceful for us.

Your words made noise stop for a while. Thank you for blessing me with your words.

I love you so,
Dad

March 3, 1991

Dear Son,

Yesterday another gem. As you, your brother, mother and sister walked you to the kindergarten around the corner, your brother fell behind.

As he caught up and expressed fear, you comforted him by saying that he need not be afraid as long as you are with him.

I sit now in church as I write, I see you seated with the family, drowsy and nearly asleep.

Now the minister speaks and I see you are awake, alert. At five years old, you are quite a young man.

Love,
Dad

March 28, 1991

Dear Son,
Things that sell can be measured by their dollar value, but important things, things of importance, have value beyond that of dollars. Important things cannot be measured in dollars.

The energies of one's life are largely expended in the pursuit of whatever it is that is treasured. That pursuit will tell you where your heart really is.

Choose carefully and wisely before you run. Don't allow petty values to be forced upon you by anyone. Principles are more important than almost anything.

Love,
Dad

Frank E. Robinson, Jr.

June 3, 1991

Dear Son,
We are moving forward in multi-ethnicity here and I am so pleased.

I see a body of every race that is not ashamed of Jesus.

While many applaud this in a philosophical sense, ethnocentric churches are the norm. Whether Eurocentric or Afrocentric, such thinking sets predetermined limitations that conflict with the mandate of Christ.

We should hate evil and injustice, as we fear the Lord and love the truth. We should love our neighbor and our enemy. The larger picture, all nations, must not escape our view. *We* are sent to *them*.

Put your hand with me to the plow and see the labor ahead. There is a promise of harvest.

Love,
Dad

PS I received the report over the phone, that your teacher caught you speaking about Jesus and intimidated you before others. A boy laughed. You were crushed. These, my son, are the ones that we are sent to. Come with me.

June 11, 1991

Dear Son,
Today you are six years old. No longer do I hear in my mind the sounds of your first cries. They have slipped past my fingertips, but it seems they are just past, just barely.

Six years ago, the day you were born, as I drove your mother to the city of your birth, I stopped to help a friend start a car. That friend passed away last year. Everyone's in transition. Seems like almost everything is coming or going as we stand on the edge of a razor in a small space called *now*.

Spring, summer, fall and winter, day and night, weeks, months and years, all are set in motion. We are getting older. So, anchor me to the Rock, a place of no change, a place of constant light. Seasons come and go. People come and go. Political ideologies rise and fall. I am going to leave this earth one day, my boy. Come, go with me to everlasting life.

I love you so much,
Dad

July 9, 1991

Dear Son,
I am at a loss at present to think of anything great that emerged from comfort. We labor and strive for a higher level of comfort and ease, but what is it of lasting weight, of true greatness that was birthed without struggle?

Reflection upon purpose and lasting good is helpful.

We are so given to entertainment in our culture. It is like a drug that intoxicates and numbs us. We pay for what we do not need.

Where is the man or woman not driven to self-enrichment, but to the enrichment and improvement of mankind? I don't see many. A new century is on the horizon and we are so comfortable.

Love,
Dad

PS Worthless things may have a dollar value. The most important things cannot be purchased with money. A poor man may be rich in love, loyalty, integrity, faith and liberty in righteousness and good conscience. A wealthy man may be utterly impoverished regarding such things. His wealth cannot secure such things. Rather, his level of comfort may insulate or isolate him from feeling the personal need for such things.

Comfort and wealth are not of themselves evil, but history has well demonstrated that they can be a great source of arrogance and self-deception.

July 13, 1991

Dear Son,
The eventuality of death is worthy of consideration.

(I began this letter on the date above, but now I continue 7-21-91). Since last Sunday, I have been near two different shootings. The most recent shooting was a very near miss. The young man's shirt was grazed, cutting two small holes in the sleeve as it sped by him.

Only God preserved our lives. Another man called me that same day. He was afraid that he might have AIDS. At the medical facility, where he was to be tested, he had lost his nerve. He called the church and I spoke to him. Calmly, kindly, I encouraged him to be tested. This man was in the torment of fear. He was terrified to take the test and terrified not to, tormented.

I am so glad that Jesus has not assigned to us such a terror. If we live, we are His. If we die, we are His. Nevertheless, we have human sentiments relative to death.

If you preceded me in death, I could scarcely bear it.

I think that I would put my face to the floor and weep until I had no more tears, trusting the Lord to comfort my heart and give me all the grace I would need to bring me through.

To lose you, for me, it would be like the major league pitcher who, in battle with cancer, lost his pitching arm. It was amputated. After its removal, the man said that he felt pain in his arm (though it no longer was there). My loss of you would be profound.

Does the earth miss the spring in winter? Do the days of cold, gray sky, of barren branches and barren earth, cry out for the days of blue skies, of warm Aprils and Mays, of singing birds and fragrant blossoms? I would miss you deeply, profoundly.

Torment and fear are not my lot. I have put my trust in the One who has conquered death.

The man I spoke of before, the one who took the AIDS test, called back yesterday. He sounded like a new man. The test was negative. A death sentence was stayed. If we live, we are the Lord's. If we die, we are the Lord's.

I reflect upon death, on human concepts and feelings of loss. Consider that God gave His son to die.

Imagine a father, giving his son to die.

God declared His love for us. Our death sentence was stayed. The bullet missed us because it struck another. Torment and fear have been dismissed. A new start has been given to men, given to you, given to me.

These words may speak to you after I have passed on to the presence of the Glorious King. We are the Lord's.

I love you, Son,
Dad

September 15, 1991

Dear Son,

These are wonderful days. Although your life has exhibited a tenderness and love for the Lord, it pleases me so much that you are grasping salvation. I have sought the Lord to give me new ideas. In recent times I have shared the Word of God with you children afresh.

I took a black stuffed animal and spoke of sin, a white stuffed animal and spoke of God and His holiness. I then took a red block and spoke about the blood of Jesus.

After these things were talked about, I went outside the door and knocked. When the door was opened for me, I spoke of Jesus desiring to be in your heart and not outside.

With understanding, you took hold of what I had shared. You later spoke of that day as the day you were saved. A day or so later, I took a toy truck and tied a jump rope to the truck and to my leg.

Then I began to talk about following Jesus. We began to fill up the truck with toy blocks. The blocks represented specific sins. When I began to walk, the overladen truck followed me.

Then I told you about confessing and forsaking sins, and attempting to cover them up. I tried to cover the blocks with my shirt. But my shirt would not conceal the loaded truck and it certainly wouldn't free me. Only by undoing the rope could I be free. The lesson was thus illustrated for you.

These days are so wonderful. You asked me the other day how could Jesus be God, because Jesus was born and God couldn't be born if He was God. So I marveled at the deep thoughts of my six year old son.

Love,
Dad

October 20, 1991

Dear Son,
Three years ago, we had a home.

The presiding officer of my denomination had taken my copyrighted artwork, published and distributed it across the nation without my consent. This greatly undermined me.

Our injury was great, for we were recovering from the desperate poverty of the South during this phase, and we had no margin with which to absorb such a loss.

But the injury has passed, the smoke has cleared, and though my hurt and humiliation were so very public, everyone can now see that I am standing on solid ground.

We are His workmanship, God's project and handiwork. In faithfulness His hand is shaping us.

Michelangelo's David was sculpted from a flawed chunk of marble that was full of possibilities. The artist carved and chipped away all that was not the masterpiece. We are God's project. In faithfulness

He carves and chips, files, sands, and refines. When the dust settles, we are like Him.

We are what He has made us to be, and we are not ashamed.

Love,
Dad

January 31, 1992

Dear Son,
This book is nearly complete. I must invest time in your brother's and sister's books. Time is short. It is my intention that this book survives me. This is part of my investment in you.

It came to me last night that I should include in your education accounts of your predecessors that are ethnically descriptive; lucid and not blurred. Your sense of personal identity is very important. A man can stand alone, if necessary, if he knows who he is, and why he is here.

Beyond that, I believe that there are some things worth dying for, worth giving one's life for.

I do not advocate foolhardiness. A wise man's heart should seek to discover purpose and timing. Frederick Douglass could have died with John Brown, but there was more to be done. Each man could have pointed to his own purpose and time.

I believe that there is a time to flee, and I have done that before. There is a time to stand, and I have done that, also.

In a sense, I have already lost my life for the things that I believe. But it is not good to allow for self-flattery in such things, and even brave men may become cowards if given the right scenario.

Perhaps in your day you may evaluate and ask yourself, "Is this the purpose, or cause, that exceeds the value of my life? Is this then the time?" Surely, you will understand in that day, should it come.

Hatred should be reserved for evil. Hate evil. The human race shares common blood. Beneath our color, hair, shape and class distinctions, is blood, human blood. Don't hate men. The defiant, hardened criminal and the grieving mother, each is someone's son and someone's daughter. Treat others and love others as you want to be treated and as you want to be loved.

You see, my son, great power is yours because you know who you are and you know where you are going. You have the power to choose so many things. Be a wise man, a man of character, of value, of worth. Come with me, my son, and taste eternity.

Lovingly,
Your father

April 30, 1992

Dear Son,
Yesterday afternoon the verdicts were read in the case of the police officers who beat a man named Rodney King. The officers beat this man as one would beat… no, even animals are seldom beat so maliciously.

It happened to be caught on video and seen around the world. None of the officers, none of them, were found guilty. LA erupted in flames, looting and violence.

A segment of our society, I think, flatters itself, denies and insulates itself from the reality of its own racist condition. But, that flattery, denial and insulation cannot withstand the weight of evidence that the world has seen. The condition is exposed. The disease is not gone.

Your brother, Josiah, was concerned for my personal safety when he returned from kindergarten earlier. He wanted to go with me wherever I went. He said, "If you get hurt, I get hurt." How profound. How noble. How brave.

In a sense, I think that any person of color who saw Mr. King's beating could say, "That could be my father, my son or my brother. That could be me!" In a symbolic sense, "That *is* me!"

Could any of those jurors see the beating from such a perspective? I think not. At least the verdicts indicate that.

I wish all of us had said, "When he got hurt, I got hurt."

May God help us all. Let us search and try our ways and turn again to the Lord.

Love,
Dad

July 10, 1992

Dear Son,
If experience is a teacher, it is also a book to be read. There are pages and passages better understood in time, as they cannot be immediately translated. We need perspective. We are so limited.

Read them diligently and grasp their meaning. Get a good understanding from your lessons in life. Apply to the present what you have learned from the past. People change, principles do not change.

People manufacture and manipulate images that are empty of substance. They are lies. The image of love for example, sells clothing, cosmetics, fast food, automobiles, and real estate. It is apparently effective in making the sale attractive. But in your heart, Son, you know that true love is deeper than that, more profound than that.

How I hate manipulation! How I love the truth! Solomon said to buy the truth and to not sell it.

Buy the truth, my son, the pilgrim, and sell it not. Keep your big eyes open. Be discerning and wise.

Love,
Dad

PS Remember that the giant Goliath only lost one fight. He tangled with a man of God who had learned from the lessons God sent his way. When it was time to fight, David ran toward his enemy. Goliath didn't know it, but he was about to die.

March 2, 1993

Dear Son,
Of the many friends that I have made, it seems that only a few can see into the identity struggles and disenfranchisement that I personally wrestle with from time to time. I suspect that your identity struggles will be even deeper than mine, due to your biracial conception. So much of that is my fault.

I have sought to not allow extraction of either ancestry from your perception of yourself. Africans came before you. Europeans and Americans came before you. You are a river, not required to denounce the various streams and creeks that caused your existence.

The issues and questions of justice and race relations are so much bigger than I am. This is bigger than me. I want to do the will of God in my generation. I'm unable to go back in time or forward in time. Only in the now can we act.

In a conversation we had the other day, I surprised your mother. I said that if I could have somehow prevented slavery by cutting off my right hand, I would do it. She attempted to correct me by saying,

"You mean your left hand," because as a skilled artist, surely my right hand could not have been meant.

But I would give my right hand. I would give my life. I would die, if that could somehow have prevented slavery and the horrors it inflicted.

Who are my people? The sons and daughters of God, they are my people. Come, take your place with me. You know my heart well enough to know these are not empty words, but truth. Don't allow the truth to be trivialized by any dilettante, any sloganeer, or any passing fellow.

Come and take your place with me. I am a father who very much loves and treasures his son. You are mine.

Love,
Dad

Son,

It is possible for a person to hate something with great intensity, and yet, in time gravitate toward that which was formerly hated.

This phenomenon can be seen or illustrated in the vile behavior of a child molester, a predator, a victimizer, who himself at one time had been an unprotected victim. Though he hated what happened to him, he now imposes the same upon others. He has now become the monstrous exporter of that which he hated.

A victim of racism can become a racist, so you must guard your heart. It would seem that the adverse experience would inoculate from the disease. Sometimes it does, sometimes it doesn't. What will you allow it to do to you?

We look to the horizon and wonder, "What does the future hold?" Are we to be optimistic of improvement and progress in this challenge, this historic and fateful struggle?

A boy standing on the deck of a ship, having just

Boarded, looked across the water and asked, "Will there be storms?"

The officer of the ship, standing nearby, put his arm around the boy and said, "There's a place you can't even see from here. That's where we are going. Storms are part of the typical passage, but only a part. Our destination is so important, so necessary that the discomfort of the passage is tolerated."

Our destination, yours and mine, is so important and so necessary, that we tolerate the discomfort of passage. I don't know the future, but I know where I'm going. Where we are going.

Life has ups and downs, uncertainties and unfairness, but they fall more into their proper perspective because my destination is known. My destination is secure. We travel together in your childhood and your youth. One day, I'll meet you over there.

Love,
Dad

"Hatred stirs up strife, but love covers all sins"
Proverbs 10:12

Dear Son,

You are a young man now, a young man I am godly proud of. I believe I will close this book of letters to you with words about courage.

As you know, I admire courage. Men – fathers - are to provide, protect and inspire. Men should live and speak the truth. But more than these basic roles, or at least in addition to these, men should show us courage.

Men should show courage to their sons and daughters. To each man's wife, to other men, to his community, his world, to generations that follow and to God, a man is to demonstrate courage.

Now, understand me, my son. It is not always courage to fight. It takes courage to walk away, to turn the other cheek and to surrender the right to revenge. It takes courage to get back up when you have been knocked down, to stand when others run.

Men are to show their sons, not only how a man faces death, but how a man faces life.

A man doesn't run away when he's afraid. He doesn't run away when it is hard. A man keeps his promises and stays there. That's courage. That's what a man does.

Do it better than I have. Show your sons and show the world. Show our God to them. Son, let them say about you, in words of deep respect and admiration, for generations after you are gone, not only, "This is how a good man faces death," but, "This is how a good man faces life."

To my mixed race son, my first born, bow your head before God and stand up among men. It is your day. It's your turn.

I have been a stranger in a strange land. This world is not my home. Be strong. Be courageous. Live the life. Die the death. I will meet you over there.

Love,
Dad

March 21, 2011

Dear Son,
Sunday before last, I heard, with my own ears, you tell me about the birth of your daughter. I cannot tell you how much that means to me. It gives me such a sense of joy and completeness.

When I was six, my mother gathered the children together to tell us she was going to have a baby, and not to tell anyone. But at six, I was so excited and happy at the news, her admonition was immediately disregarded. I jumped on my little bicycle and rode around the neighborhood, telling everyone I saw, "My mom's gonna have a baby!"

The morning you told me of Ember's birth, I stopped at a gas station on our way to church. I walked in the door, threw up my hands and announced, "My granddaughter was born today!"

You are overseas now, but we anticipate getting to know this precious girl.

I listened as you told me how she is attuned to your voice, that when her eyes were covered as she was being treated for jaundice, you soothed her with your voice. You told me you said things to her like, "We are all here. Everything is OK. You are safe. You are loved. There is nothing to be afraid of. I am right here…"

The proverb tells us, "Children's children are the crown of old men and the glory of children are their fathers." I can hear Father God speak to me and to us through your words to your daughter, who cannot yet understand language. She is made to understand love in your presence.

I tried to be a good father, to learn from the flaws and mistakes of my fathers before me. Now I want you to be a great husband, a great father and a great man. Humble is the way.

I love you so much. We are all here. Everything is OK. You are safe. You are loved. There is nothing to be afraid of. I am right here…

Love,
Dad